DRAGONFLY

Aimée M. Bissonette

illustrated by
Catherine Pearson

Albert Whitman & Company
Chicago, Illinois

We've been here three hundred million years. We are small now, but back then our wings spread more than 2 feet across. And we ruled the sky.

The gigantic dragonflies that lived long ago had wingspans of up to 30 inches. They had sharp chewing mouthparts and preyed on insects and small animals that lived on land and in water.

Biologists think they were so large because there was more oxygen in the air. This made the dragonflies' breathing tubes work better and helped them grow.

We are called naiads—meaning "of the water." We start life in eggs laid on floating plants, soft moss, or the water itself. As eggs, we are helpless. Tiny, tasty morsels for fish, newts, and toads.

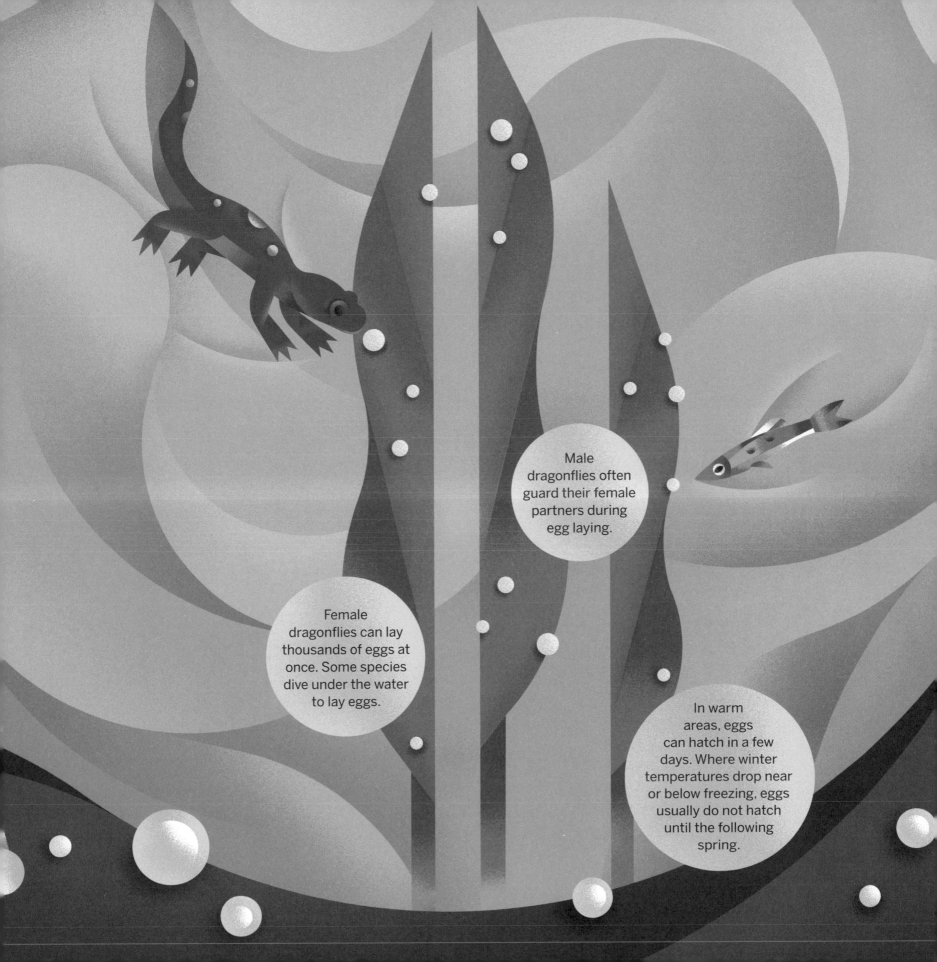

Male dragonflies often guard their female partners during egg laying.

Female dragonflies can lay thousands of eggs at once. Some species dive under the water to lay eggs.

In warm areas, eggs can hatch in a few days. Where winter temperatures drop near or below freezing, eggs usually do not hatch until the following spring.

It's a dangerous time for us. We need to hatch.

If we do, we join the other pond dwellers in the sun-filtered depths. Tadpoles, fish, caddis flies. A whole watery world. A watery world where we swim and dive and hunt our food.

Though small and not fully formed, nymphs are still good underwater predators.

Drab in color, they blend in with the underwater world.

Nymphs need to grow to avoid being eaten, so they prey on worms, guppies— even other nymphs.

In the water, we eat and eat. Our tiny nymph bodies grow. Over and over we split our skins— nine times, twelve times, seventeen. With each change of skin, we get larger and stronger.

Most of a dragonfly's life is underwater, catching and eating prey. Nymphs are skilled hunters. Fang-like pincers help them snatch prey quickly.

Nymphs shed their skins multiple times as they grow. As a nymph grows, its body pushes against the outer skin until it splits. This process is called molting.

About halfway through molting, the nymph's future wings appear. After that, the wings grow quickly.

It usually takes one to three years for a nymph to become an adult, although it can take up to eight years with some dragonfly species.

We spend the longest parts of our lives in the water preparing for what we will become. Until it is time and we crawl out from the wild wet.

How quickly nymphs grow depends on the temperature of the water and how much food is available. In warm waters, a new generation of dragonflies may emerge each year. In cooler waters, where food is scarcer, it may take several years.

A day or two before the nymph leaves the water, it goes into a state of rest. Then it makes the final changes to its exoskeleton, usually early in the morning.

The nymph moves to shallow water. It stops feeding. Its wing pads swell. Its adult color patterns start to show under its skin. It starts to breathe air. It gets ready to crawl out of the water.

Time to crack open our sturdy skins, and free our bodies, legs, and wings from their cramped casings. One gooey wing. Two. Three. Four. Wings spread wide to dry in the air, our water days behind us.

At last, the nymph crawls out of the water onto a plant or dry rock and molts one last time. It slowly expands to its full size. It is a dragonfly now, ready to fly in a few short hours when its wings dry.

Dragonflies are weak fliers until their bodies harden. It's a risky time for them. Birds, spiders, ants, and other predators eat many young dragonflies in the first few days after they emerge.

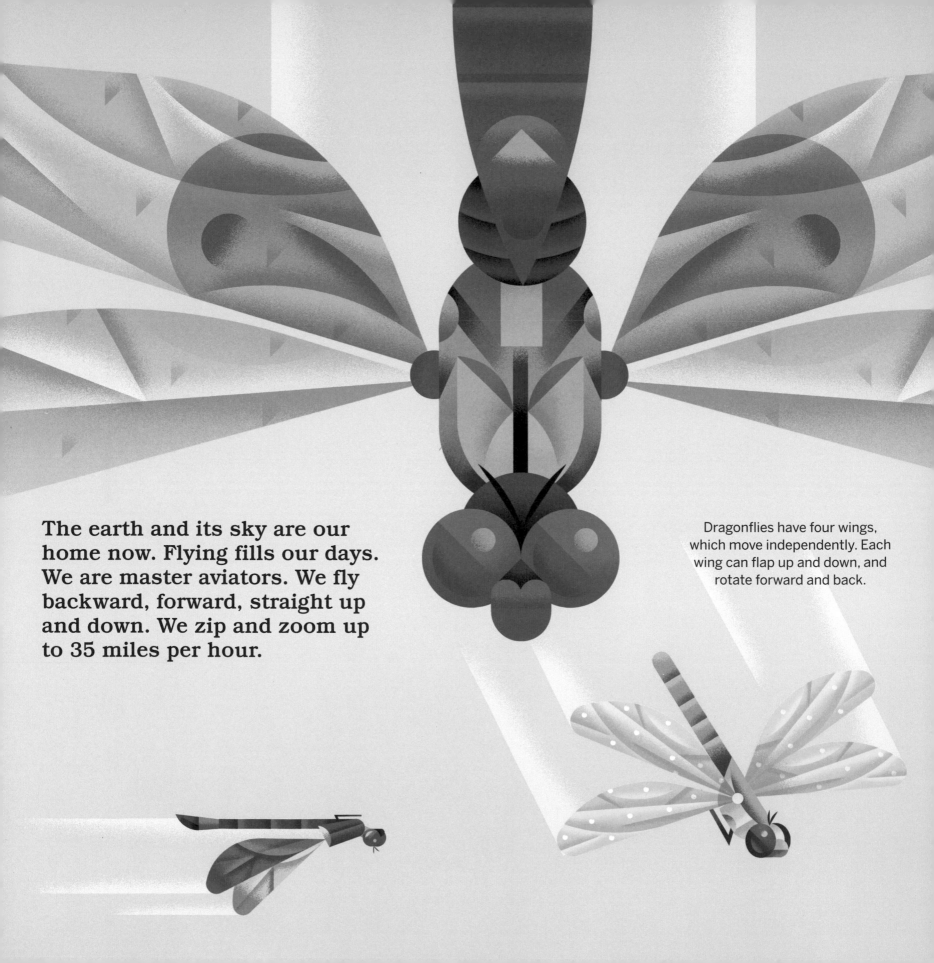

The earth and its sky are our home now. Flying fills our days. We are master aviators. We fly backward, forward, straight up and down. We zip and zoom up to 35 miles per hour.

Dragonflies have four wings, which move independently. Each wing can flap up and down, and rotate forward and back.

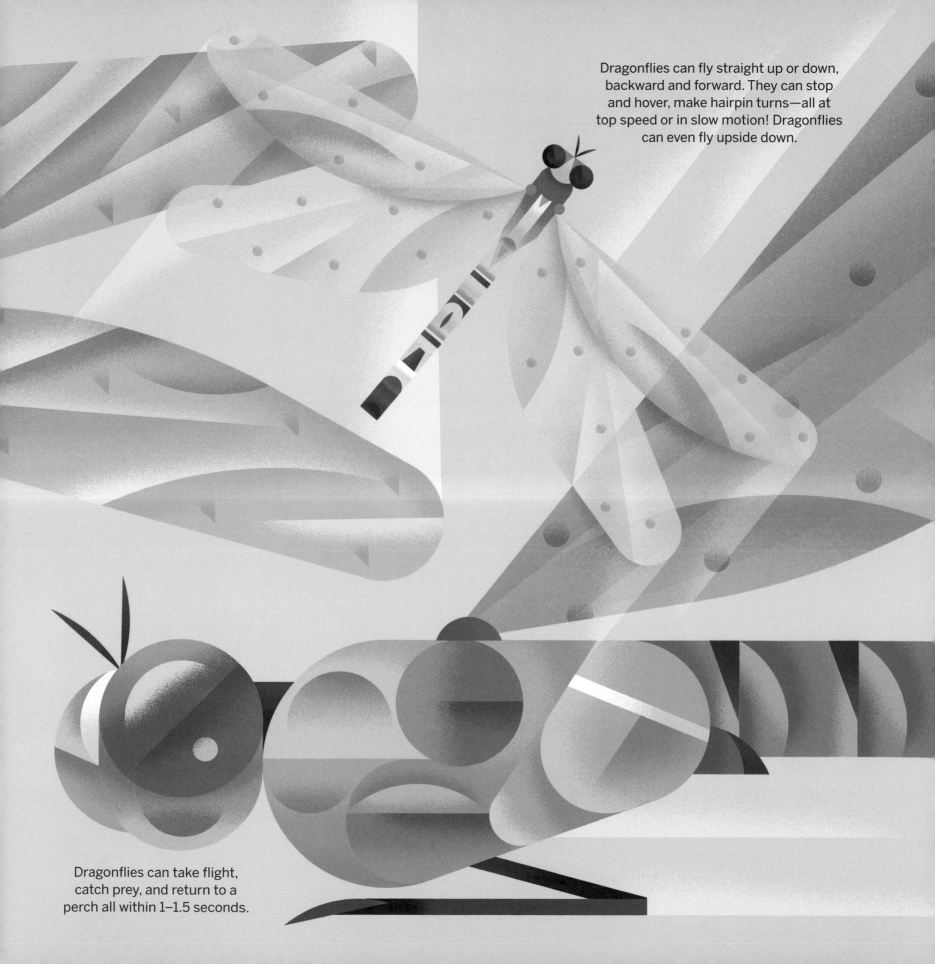

Dragonflies can fly straight up or down, backward and forward. They can stop and hover, make hairpin turns—all at top speed or in slow motion! Dragonflies can even fly upside down.

Dragonflies can take flight, catch prey, and return to a perch all within 1–1.5 seconds.

As we fly, we feed. Our bodies yearn for insect food. Flies, moths, mosquitoes—especially mosquitoes. We fly low through the grasses. We dart left and right. It's a game of cat and mouse, until at last we're within reach. Then...

STRIKE, BITE, GRIND, SWALLOW!

Bug after bug. Hundreds each day.

Dragonflies hold their spiky legs like baskets, catching their prey as they fly. They also fly through swarms of insects with their mouths gaping open. Their jaws can open as wide as their whole head. They can eat their own weight in insects in 30 minutes.

Dragonflies capture more than 90 percent of their prey. But they don't chase their prey; they intercept it. They figure out where their prey is going to be by judging the distance, speed, and direction of their prey. Then they fly to that spot.

Warm days and clear, clean water. That's the recipe for a dragonfly's life. We perch on the long stems of waving grasses. We skim low across ponds.

Dragonflies rest in the sun to save energy when they aren't looking for food or a mate. They also rest after eating, with their wings held open.

Dragonflies are cold-blooded, which means they need external heat to stay warm. The muscles that flap their wings must be kept warm. They can whir their wings in flight, and they try to face the sun. They even use their wings as reflectors to trap sunlight.

Our bodies shimmer in the sun—
ruby red, emerald green, amber, blue,
gold—a rainbow of colors.

Dragonfly colors range from metallic
to pastel. They are iridescent,
meaning they seem to change color
when seen from different angles.

Some dragonfly wings are transparent
and look glassy, while others are
brightly colored. Sometimes wings are
spotted or banded.

We are not one kind, but thousands of different kinds: pondhawks, emperors, shadowdragons, boghaunters. We are found nearly everywhere. Lakes, ponds, mountains—even desert pools.

There are about 3,000 species of dragonflies. About three hundred live in the United States. They live on every continent except Antarctica, from sea level up to the mountains.

Wherever we are, we soar. Summer is our time to shine. The natural world is our playground. A playground we share with the birds and fish, beaver and snakes—whatever is overhead and underfoot. Until...

Adult dragonflies can also be prey: for water bugs, frogs, fish, birds, spiders, lizards—even larger species of dragonflies. Their best defense is escape. Their big eyes and incredible flying skills save them.

It happens. Summer ends. Autumn winds chill the air. Dry leaves float down from overhanging branches, and we're gone.

Dragonflies have short lives. Some live only a week or two as adults, while others last a few months. They cannot live in cold weather. When winter comes, they can no longer survive.

But dragonfly nymphs are alive and hunting under the ice in streams and ponds. They grow all winter and emerge as adults in spring. Dragonflies lay many eggs. There will be enough dragonflies to continue to rule the sky.

But we've been here three hundred million years. We are naiads—of the water. And we laid our eggs on floating plants, soft moss, and the water itself.

We'll be back.

Author's Note

Dragonflies are carnivorous insects, meaning they feed on other creatures. They were some of the first winged insects to evolve, and scientists have found evidence of very large prehistoric dragonflies. Today's dragonflies are much smaller, with wingspans ranging from 0.5–7.5 inches.

Dragonflies' colors and markings are spectacular. Dragonflies live all over the world but are almost always found near ponds and streams.

Despite their sharp teeth, dragonflies do not sting or bite people. In fact, because dragonflies need clean water to live and grow, it's always good to see them. Dragonflies are a sign of a healthy environment.

Resources

activities

Biggs, Kathy and Tim Manolis. *Dragonflies of North America: A Color and Learn Book with Activities.* Sebastopol, CA: Azalea Creek, 2007.

Thompson, Ami. *Dragonfly Curriculum Guide.* Self-published, CreateSpace, 2013.

books for children

Earley, Chris. *Dragonflies: Catching, Identifying, How and Where They Live.* Richmond Hill, ON: Firefly Books, 2013.

Glaser, Linda. *Dazzling Dragonflies: A Life Cycle Story.* Minneapolis: Millbrook, 2008.

books for adults

Nikula, Blair and Jackie Sones. *Stokes Beginner's Guide to Dragonflies.* Boston: Little, Brown, 2002.

Paulson, Dennis. *Dragonflies & Damselflies: A Natural History.* Princeton, NJ: Princeton University Press, 2019.

With huge thanks to Susan and Annette,
such talented, nature-loving friends!
And, as always, with love to Bryan.—AMB

To Stefan, for all of his support, advice, and love.
Thank you for always being by my side.—CP

Library of Congress Cataloging-in-Publication data is on file with the publisher.
Text copyright © 2020 Aimée M. Bissonette
Illustrations copyright © 2020 by Albert Whitman & Company
Illustrations by Catherine Pearson
First published in the United States of America in 2020 by Albert Whitman & Company

ISBN 978-0-8075-5821-8 (hardcover)
ISBN 978-0-8075-5822-5 (ebook)

Printed in China

10 9 8 7 6 5 4 3 2 1 WKT 24 23 22 21 20

Design by Rick DeMonico

For more information about Albert Whitman & Company,
visit our website at www.albertwhitman.com